Each Inner Workbook is a self-study retreat or workshop that you can do at home. They are designed to become a part of your day, just like that first cup of tea, and invite you to journal the experience as you develop your practice, making it your own.

Contents

Introduction
02

Week 1: Dream Awareness
16

Week 2: All in the Details
32

Week 3: Dream Guides
48

Week 4: Deeper Consciousness
64

About the Author
80

Introduction

What is *Dreamwork?*

Hello dreamer!
Welcome to the journey
into your dreams.

DREAMWORK IS THE FASCINATING voyage into the realms of your own consciousness, an exploration of the rich tapestry of dreams that unfolds while you sleep. It's like diving into a hidden treasure chest within your mind, where each dream holds the potential for profound insights and revelations. Through the practice of dreamwork, you open the door to a world of mystery and magic, where your unconscious mind reveals its secrets in the language of symbols and imagery.

I hold the belief that dreams serve as manifestations of consciousness. Consciousness, in essence, embodies your individual awareness and interpretation of reality, surroundings and encounters. It encompasses your sensory perceptions, emotional responses, bodily sensations and cognitive processes.

While many associate consciousness solely with being in a wakeful state, its scope extends far beyond. Consciousness can also manifest in dreams, memories, comatose states, trance states, daydreams and psychedelic experiences. These instances are classified as 'Altered States of Consciousness', diverging from the conventional awake and sober perception. Nevertheless, they represent valid forms of consciousness, rooted in the realm of perception.

> **❝❞**
> Dreams come to tell us something about OUR LIVES that WE have been missing.
> — James Redfield

Simply because dreams exist in a realm separate from waking reality does not diminish their impact on our subjective experience. The implications of this are exciting because the more you engage with your dreams, the more you explore and expand your consciousness.

Dreams are our teachers. They should not be shrugged off as silly nightly reveries or junk data; but embraced as personal experiences of consciousness that hold valuable messages to help us live a better life.

Introduction

Why *develop* a conscious *dreaming practice?*

Embarking on a conscious dreaming practice is like embarking on a thrilling adventure of self-discovery and growth.

IT'S A JOURNEY into the depths of your own psyche, where you can unravel the mysteries of your unconscious mind and tap into your inner wisdom. By engaging in inner work through dreams, you can gain a deeper understanding of yourself, unlock your creativity and cultivate a sense of spiritual connection.

Dreams offer a unique opportunity to explore unresolved emotions, fears and wounds and to receive guidance and healing for navigating the challenges of waking life. Your unconscious mind becomes your guide.

As you explore the landscapes of your dreams, you become more attuned to the subtle nuances of your inner world. There you will find creative potential, chances to problem solve and ways to transcend challenges. This heightened awareness allows you to navigate your consciousness with greater ease and intention, leading to a more integrated and fulfilling experience of life.

By doing the inner work of understanding your consciousness as you sleep, you can also begin to comprehend the nature of reality and your place within it. As you explore the boundless realms of your dreams, you come to realize the interconnectedness of all things and the infinite possibilities that exist within the universe. This expanded perspective can foster a sense of awe and wonder, enriching your understanding of the world and your place within it.

Moreover, cultivating awareness of your dreams can have a profound impact on your waking life. As you become more conscious and aware of your dreams, you naturally become more conscious and aware in your daily life. This heightened state of awareness allows you to approach life with greater mindfulness and presence, leading to more meaningful and fulfilling experiences. The mundane aspects of life take on a new sense of magic and wonder, as you recognize the beauty and significance inherent in every moment. When you dream with lucidity, you live a more lucid life.

In essence, developing a conscious dreaming practice is a transformative journey that leads to greater self-awareness, expanded consciousness and a deeper connection to the world around you. By embracing the mysteries of your dreams, you unlock the hidden potential within yourself and cultivate a more integrated and joyful existence. Let's get dreaming!

Introduction

When can it be *helpful* to pay *closer attention* to *your dreams?*

PAYING CLOSER ATTENTION to your dreams can be immensely beneficial in many aspects of life. Whether you're facing major life decisions, grappling with personal struggles or simply seeking inspiration and guidance, dreams can provide valuable insights and perspectives. They offer a safe space to explore your deepest thoughts and emotions and can offer comfort and healing during times of stress or uncertainty. By cultivating a mindful awareness of your dreams, you can harness their power to support and guide you on your journey through life.

Many of us have experienced major life changes such as the death of a loved one, divorce or relationship problems and our nightly dreams can offer solace and insight. During times of grief or emotional upheaval, dreams may provide a space for processing emotions, gaining clarity and finding comfort in symbolic imagery and messages. During times of stress or uncertainty, such as job loss, starting a new job or experiencing illness or injury, dreams can offer a sense of perspective and resilience. Your dream imagery during challenging life chapters may reflect underlying fears or anxieties, providing an opportunity for self-reflection and emotional processing.

If you are navigating significant life events such as pregnancy, becoming a parent or empty nesting, dreams can offer guidance and support as you transition into new roles and responsibilities. Dreams may reflect your hopes, fears and aspirations, helping you navigate the complexities of parenthood and family dynamics. Even during seemingly mundane or routine experiences such as going on holiday or organizing a complicated event, dreams can provide valuable insights and creative solutions.

Similarly, when embarking on a new spiritual or material chapter in life, dreams can serve as a source of guidance and direction. Whether exploring new beliefs or pursuing new opportunities, dreams may offer rewarding insights into the best path forwards and help you align with your higher purpose or goals.

If you are creative, you can harvest your dreams for inspiration and problem-solving ideas. Whether you're an artist, musician, writer or simply seeking creative inspiration, dreams can provide a wealth of imaginative content and innovative solutions.

Many renowned artists and thinkers throughout history have credited their dreams with inspiring their greatest works.

In essence, paying attention to your dreams can be helpful in virtually every aspect of life. Each night, your dreams offer guidance, inspiration and healing during times of transition, growth and challenge. As well as creative inspiration, emotional support and problem-solving ideas. Dreams have the power to illuminate your path forward and enrich your lived experience.

I have recorded each of the meditations included in the workbook for you to listen to.

https://innerworkproject.com/product/dreamwork/

66 99
DREAMS are the royal road to the UNCONSCIOUS.
Sigmund Freud

Introduction

Ways of interpreting your dreams: *a short history*

THROUGHOUT HISTORY, humans have been fascinated by the mysteries of dreams and have sought to interpret their meanings and significance. Dream interpretation has been practised by cultures around the world for millennia, with ancient civilizations using dreams as a source of guidance, inspiration and spiritual insight. From the dream temples of Ancient Greece to the teachings of Freud and Jung by way of modern psychology, the study of dreams has evolved and adapted over time. Today, there are countless methods and approaches to dream interpretation, ranging from the symbolic analysis of archetypes to the psychological exploration of the unconscious mind.

In Ancient Egypt, dreams held great significance, with Egyptians believing that dreams were a means of communication between the mortal realm and the divine. Dream interpreters, known as 'masters of secret things' were consulted to decipher the symbolic language of dreams and unveil their hidden meanings. Dreams were also seen as portals to the spiritual realm, offering insights into the future or guidance from the gods.

Similarly, in Ancient Greece, dreams were viewed as divine messages from the gods, offering guidance, warnings or prophecies. Greek philosophers, Plato and Aristotle pondered the nature of dreams and their relationship to the unconscious mind, laying the groundwork for later theories of dream interpretation.

In the Middle Ages, dreams were often interpreted through the lens of religion and superstition, with Christian theologians viewing dreams as either divine revelations or temptations from the devil. Dream interpretation became intertwined with religious beliefs, with dreams serving as a means of communicating with God or receiving spiritual guidance.

During the Renaissance, interest in dreams and their interpretation saw a resurgence, with scholars and philosophers delving into the symbolic language of dreams. The Swiss psychiatrist Carl Jung, a pioneering figure in the field of psychology, explored the concept of archetypes and the collective unconscious, proposing that dreams contain universal symbols and themes that reflect deeper aspects of the human psyche.

> The dream is the SMALL HIDDEN DOOR in the deepest and most INTIMATE SANCTUM of the SOUL.
> Carl Jung

In the modern era, dream interpretation has evolved into a multidisciplinary field, drawing insights from psychology, neuroscience, anthropology and other disciplines. Sigmund Freud, the founder of psychoanalysis, developed a theory of dream interpretation that emphasized the role of the unconscious mind and the significance of dream symbolism. According to Freud, dreams are expressions of repressed desires and wishes, serving as a means of wish-fulfilment.

Today, dream analysis techniques such as free association, journaling and active imagination are used to uncover the latent meaning of dreams and gain insights into the dreamer's unconscious mind.

The interpretation of dreams is a deeply personal and subjective process, shaped by individual beliefs, experiences and perspectives. This is the beauty of the four-week journey in this workbook. You will be exploring the rich symbolism, imagery, narrative and emotional content of your dreams, and by doing so you will gain a deeper understanding of yourself and your inner world. You will begin to unlock the mysteries of your unconscious mind and tap into your inner wisdom. Let's do the inner work!

Types of Dreams

Dream *categories*

DREAMS COME IN A MYRIAD of forms, each with their own unique characteristics and meanings. From vivid and fantastical dreams that transport you to other worlds, to subtle and symbolic dreams that convey important messages, there's no shortage of variety in the dream realm. Dreams can be mystical and even prophetic, reflecting future events or hidden truths, or they can be reflective, mirroring your thoughts, feelings and experiences from waking life. By familiarizing yourself with the different types of dreams, you can better understand their significance and interpret their messages with greater clarity. Let's unlock their mysteries.

Compensatory dreams
These dreams often serve to balance out or compensate for waking life experiences. For example, if you repress feelings of anger during the day, your dreams may act out with violent content. Compensatory dreams can help restore emotional equilibrium and can act as prompts to focus on areas of life that need self-care.

Precognitive dreams
Also known as prophetic dreams, these experiences involve dreaming about events or situations that later come true in waking life. While the mechanism behind precognitive dreams remains a mystery, many people report having dreams that seem to foreshadow future events. These dreams can be unsettling or intriguing, depending on their content and significance.

Nightmares
These dreams are often intense and frightening and can evoke feelings of fear, anxiety or distress. They often involve scenarios of danger, threat or harm and can leave a lasting impression on the dreamer. Nightmares may arise from unresolved fears or trauma, and may serve as a way for the subconscious mind to process difficult emotions or experiences. These dreams can be our biggest teachers as they point towards an area within that needs healing.

Recurring dreams
These are dreams that occur repeatedly over time, often featuring similar themes, settings or characters. Recurring dreams may reflect unresolved issues or conflicts in the dreamer's life and may offer valuable insights into recurring patterns or themes. By paying attention to recurring dreams, you can gain a deeper understanding of your unconscious fears, trauma, desires or aspirations.

Lucid dreams
These are phenomenal dreams in which the dreamer becomes aware that they are dreaming while still in the dream. This awareness allows the dreamer to consciously interact with and willingly participate within the dream environment, leading to a sense of co-creation and empowerment. Lucid dreaming can be a powerful tool for self-exploration, creativity, insights, personal growth and mystical experiences.

Progressive dreams
These are a style of dream that unfolds in a linear or chronological manner, often following a narrative structure. These dreams may involve a sense of progression or development, with events unfolding over time. Progressive dreams can offer insights into the dreamer's unconscious journey of the soul, problem-solving, goals and potentially providing guidance for navigating life's challenges and opportunities.

Anxiety dreams
These commonly shared dreams can evoke feelings of stress, worry or unease. They often involve scenarios or situations that reflect the dreamer's fears, insecurities or anxieties. Anxiety dreams may serve as a way for the unconscious mind to process and release pent-up tension or negative emotion, and may offer opportunities for personal insight and growth.

Grief dreams
Also known as 'after death visitation dreams', this dreaming phenomenon is often experienced by those who are mourning the loss of a loved one. They commonly involve encounters or interactions with the deceased, providing a sense of comfort, closure or even distress. They can serve as a means of processing emotions, grappling with unresolved issues or finding solace amidst the pain of loss.

> ❝❞
> We are all MADE of dreams.
> Shakespeare

Prodromal dreams

These are somewhat rare and exceptional dreams that provide early warning signs or indicators of health issues within your own body. Recognizing a prodromal dream can help you listen to the messages that your body is sending you through dreams and therefore help you to take proactive steps to safeguard or improve your health.

Sleep paralysis

This is a sleep phenomenon in which the dreamer experiences temporary paralysis upon waking or falling asleep. During sleep paralysis, you may be unable to move or speak, and could experience hallucinations or sensations of vibrations, electricity, pressure or suffocation. Sleep paralysis can be a frightening and disorienting experience, often accompanied by feelings of fear or panic, which in return can highlight areas of life that need attention.

False awakening dreams

These occur when the dreamer dreams that they have woken up from sleep, only to realize later that they are still dreaming. False awakening dreams can be confusing and disorienting, blurring the line between dreams and reality. However, they may serve as a reminder of the fluid and subjective nature of perception and may prompt the dreamer to question their assumptions about reality and consciousness. This is a great opportunity to explore lucid dreaming.

By identifying and understanding your various dream categories and paying attention to their content and significance, you can then identify and understand what's happening in your unconscious realms. As you keep your dream diary over the next four weeks, you can begin to decipher the types of dreams you are having and how they might connect with your day-to-day experiences as well as the 'bigger picture' of your life – your inner dreams and aspirations, emotional healing and releasing, spiritual awakening or personal growth. **Let's dream on!**

> **Hope is a WAKING DREAM.**
> **Aristotle**

Symbolism & *meaning*

Dreams are like puzzles. They are filled with symbols and imagery that hold hidden meanings and messages. By deciphering these symbols and understanding their significance, you can reveal the deeper truths and wisdom contained within your dreams. From common symbols like animals, objects and places, to recurring themes, each element of your dreams carries its own symbolic weight.

One of the key benefits of exploring the symbolism and meaning of your dreams is the opportunity to uncover your personal mythology. Just as cultures and civilizations have their own myths and legends that reflect their collective values and beliefs, individuals have their own personal mythology that shapes their worldview and understanding of themselves. Through dreamwork, you can delve into the symbolic language of your dreams to uncover the archetypal themes and motifs that help bring meaning, guidance and clarity to your life journey.

By paying attention to recurring symbols and themes in your dreams, you can begin to piece together the narrative of your personal mythology. For example, recurring symbols such as water, bridges or snakes may carry specific meanings and associations for you, reflecting your inner struggles, wounds or unresolved conflicts. By recognizing these symbols and exploring their significance in the context of your life, you can access the underlying patterns that shape your thoughts, emotions and behaviours. You then have the power to make the necessary changes in your waking life to be a happier and more emotionally integrated person.

Exploring the symbolism of dreams can also help you navigate the challenges and transitions of life. Dreams often reflect our unconscious concerns and anxieties, offering clues into unsettled trauma or areas of growth. For example, a dream about being lost in a maze may symbolize feelings of confusion or uncertainty in waking life, while a dream about flying may represent a need for freedom or transcendence.

You can learn to interpret these symbols and decode their messages, gaining clarity and perspective on your waking experiences. By engaging in reflective practices such as journaling, meditation or creative expression, you can deepen your understanding of your dreams, allowing you to integrate their wisdom into your daily life. Let's unlock their mysteries!

Introduction

How to *use* this *workbook*

THIS WORKBOOK and dream journal is crafted with the intention of facilitating your journey towards a deeper connection with your dreams, fostering growth and the evolution of your consciousness in both your dreaming and waking states.

See it as a map for your journey into dreamwork. I will be providing guidance, exercises and prompts to help you recall, explore and interpret your dreams. Use this resource as a tool for self-reflection and introspection, recording your dreams, thoughts, experiences and insights along the way.

By engaging with the exercises and reflections in this workbook, you will deepen your understanding of your dreams and their significance in your life. You will even get to know yourself a bit better. As the Ancient Greek philosopher Socrates once said: 'know thyself'. This remains a timeless reminder of the value of introspection and self-awareness in leading a fulfilling life.

Conscious dreaming isn't just sitting back and watching the show. It's diving headfirst into the wild ride of your own consciousness. It is a quest for self-discovery.

Over the course of four weeks, I will walk alongside you as your dream guide. Together we will dive into the depths of your inner world and I will guide you through the process of uncovering what lies beneath the surface of your waking reality; leading you through daily and nightly interactions with your dreams.

✶ In **Week 1**, we focus on increasing dream awareness, from creating a 'dream space' and bedtime rituals to dream mantras and dream recall.
✶ **Week 2** delves into the details of your dreams – the people, places, patterns and symbols that show up in your dreams as clues.
✶ In **Week 3**, we explore your dreams as guides; how to connect the dots between your dreams and your daily life, how dreams can help you deepen your intuition and how guides can show up in your dreams.
✶ And in **Week 4**, you will be ready to start exploring your dreams as a wellspring of creativity, and a pathway to emotional healing and manifesting your inner heart's desires.

I have included dream journaling pages throughout so that you can record your dreams, thoughts, feelings, questions and intentions. You might only have the faintest thread of a dream to start with, but as you write down your nightly experiences you will find it easier to recall details and in time will begin to see some interesting patterns emerging.

Likewise, to begin with, you might find your dreams baffling with no significant meaning. It's ok not to immediately understand what they mean. This is why I encourage you to journal how you felt in the dream, rather than always focussing solely on what happened. Throughout this dreamwork journey, hold these two questions lightly:
How did you feel in the dream?
What does it mean for you?

With so much information at our fingertips in today's world, it can be tempting to search online for the meaning of our dreams, and that can indeed be helpful and illuminating. But I encourage you to explore what your dreams mean to you first, and then go ahead and explore other resources.

Designed to equip you with essential tools, you will begin to bridge the gap between your conscious and unconscious realms, inviting inspiration, guidance, healing, discovery, clarity,

integration, synchronicity, creativity and magic into your everyday life. Throughout the four weeks, you will need to cultivate certain qualities and attributes, including commitment, focus, discipline, playfulness, imagination, mindfulness, diligence, consistency, conscious awareness, intent, willpower and the willingness to embrace new habits and think outside of the box. These qualities will serve as the building blocks of your dreamwork practice. Embrace this adventure with an open mind and a curious and playful spirit.

Don't be too hard on yourself as it will block your progress. Be gentle and, most importantly, have fun.
Let your journey begin!

Week 1

dream
awa

Week 1 Dream Awareness

Day 1 Dream journaling

One of the easiest ways that you can enhance your ability to remember your dreams is to simply write them down upon awakening.

Incorporating dream journaling into your bedtime routine can help strengthen the connection to your dreams.

This is an important foundation to dreamwork. Keep this journal and a pen by your bedside, which will allow you to capture dream imagery, emotions and insights as soon as you wake up, reinforcing the connection between waking and dreaming consciousness.

When you remember a dream, even a few fragments, give it a title. Make a note of any details, objects, settings, places and feelings. As you keep your dream journal over the next weeks, and beyond, you can consider the types of dreams you experience (see page 10) and how they relate to both your day-to-day and the bigger picture of your life.

Writing down your dreams not only helps to improve your dream memory recall; this practice also helps to activate more dreams.

Before you go to sleep tonight, write down a dream from the past.

❝❞
DREAMS are the bridge to our inner worlds, offering PROFOUND INSIGHTS and guiding us towards SELF-DISCOVERY and HEALING.
Tree Carr

DREAM DIARY

Dream title.

Dream type.

Dream notes.
setting / feelings / objects / people / thoughts / narrative

This dream made me feel...

Question.
Does the dream relate to any current themes in my life?

Dreamwork

Week 1 Dream Awareness

Day 2 Creating a dream space

Let's get started with creating your dream space. This is more than just setting up a bedroom for sleep: it's about crafting an environment that nurtures both restful slumber and more connected dreaming. The layout, decor and ambience of your bedroom can significantly impact your consciousness, well-being and connection to dreams. I like to see the bedroom as a sacred dream space, primed to transport you to the dream-a-verse!

> **❝❞**
> Your BEDROOM should be a sancturay of TRANQUILITY and COMFORT.
> **Tree Carr**

First and foremost, your bedroom should be a sanctuary of tranquility and comfort. Optimal sleep conditions include a comfortable mattress and pillows, breathable bedding and appropriate room temperature and ventilation. These physical elements promote restorative sleep, allowing the mind to enter deeper states of relaxation conducive to dreaming. Invest in your sleep-care.

In addition to physical comfort, the aesthetics of the bedroom play a crucial role in creating a dream-friendly environment. Choose calming colours and soft lighting to evoke a sense of serenity. Incorporate elements of nature, such as plants or artwork inspired by the natural world, to deepen your connection to nature, which can enhance dream imagery and symbolism. Create a beautiful space.

Clutter and distractions should be minimized to create a clear and tranquil space for your mind to unwind. Keep your bedroom tidy and organized, free from electronic devices or other stimuli that may disrupt sleep or inhibit dream recall. De-junk your space.

DREAM DIARY

Dream title.

Dream type.

Dream notes.
setting / feelings / objects / people / thoughts / narrative

This dream made me feel...

Question.
What did I do yesterday and how did I feel? Does the dream correlate to my day?

Question.
Does the dream relate to any current themes in my life?

Week 1 Dream Awareness

Day 3 Dream mantras

There is power in words and affirmations! Embracing the practice of dream mantras can be a powerful tool for enhancing dreamwork and deepening your connection to your unconscious realm. Dream mantras are affirmations or intentions that you repeat to yourself, within your mind before falling asleep, setting the stage for transformative dream experiences.

The process begins with crafting your dream mantra, which may be a simple affirmation or intention related to your dream goals. This could be something like, 'I am open to receiving clear and vivid dreams,' or, 'I am lucid and aware within my dreams.' By infusing your mantra with positive energy and intention, you create a pathway for your unconscious mind to follow during sleep. It's a little like self-hypnosis.

As you drift into the transitional phase between wakefulness and sleep, reciting your dream mantra can serve as a beacon guiding you into the dream world. This liminal threshold is a fertile ground for creative exploration and deepening awareness, making it an ideal time to reinforce your intentions and affirmations.

Your dream mantra will act as a seed planted in the fertile soil of your unconscious mind, blossoming into vibrant dreamscapes and lucid adventures. It will also increase the likelihood of more deeply connected dreaming, improving dream memory recall, and paving the way for lucid moments of self-awareness within the dream itself.

What is your dream mantra? Make a note of it.

DREAM DIARY

Dream title.

Dream type.

Dream notes.
setting / feelings / objects / people / thoughts / narrative

This dream made me feel...

Question.
What did I do yesterday and how did I feel? Does the dream correlate to my day?

Question.
Does the dream relate to any current themes in my life?

Week 1 Dream Awareness

Day 4 Bedtime rituals

Engaging in evening activities that stimulate creativity and imagination can inspire and motivate dream exploration. Reading literature, listening to music or practising artistic pursuits can enrich your dream experience by providing material for the unconscious mind to draw upon during sleep. Get creative!

Participating in relaxation techniques before sleep can help quiet your mind and prepare for dreaming. Practices such as mindful breathing, progressive muscle relaxation or Yin Yoga can reduce stress and tension, allowing your mind to enter a more receptive state for dreaming. Get relaxed!

Creating a soothing environment in your sacred dream space is also key to enhancing dream connection. Dimming the lights, playing calming music or binaural beats and incorporating aromatherapy with essential oils like lavender can promote relaxation and prepare the journey for deeper dreaming. Get dreamy!

Plant allies can also be quite helpful for your nightly dream rituals. Oneirogens, or dream herbs, are natural plant-based substances that have been used for centuries to enhance dream experiences.

Drinking a nightly tea made from oneirogenic herbs like Mugwort or Blue Lotus while repeating your mantra allows you to immerse yourself in a state of receptivity and openness, inviting the magic of dreams to unfold. Choose a dream herb!

Note down your bedtime ritual here:

DREAM DIARY

Dream title.

Dream type.

Dream notes.
setting / feelings / objects / people / thoughts / narrative

This dream made me feel...

Question.
What did I do yesterday and how did I feel? Does the dream correlate to my day?

Question.
Does the dream relate to any current themes in my life?

Week 1 Dream Awareness

Day 5 Daytime mindfulness

What did you dream about last night? Trying to remember your dreams is one of the challenges of dreamwork but, there are ways to improve your dream memory recall in your new daily routines.

Beyond the physical environment, cultivating a dream-friendly mindset is essential for deepening the connection to dreams. Practices such as meditation, mindfulness and journaling can help to quiet your mind, enhance self-awareness and nurture a deeper connection to your dream world.

A gentle reminder to keep your dream journal and pen by your bedside, and as soon as you wake up, write down any fragments or details from your dreams. Include sensory impressions, emotions and any significant symbols or themes. Regularly recording your dreams reinforces the connection between waking and dreaming consciousness, making it easier to remember and analyze your dream experiences.

Another gentle reminder: setting your evening intentions before going to bed as well as using your dream mantra will also help improve your dream memory recall. Be consistent with your intentions and mantra each night. They are powerful for achieving and manifesting your dream goals.

Cultivating mindfulness and self-awareness throughout the day will enhance your dream memory recall. Take time to reflect on your experiences, emotions and thoughts, as well as any dream fragments or symbols that may arise in your waking life. By cultivating a deeper connection to your inner world, you become more attuned to the subtle cues and patterns of your dreams.

> **❝❞**
> To pay ATTENTION,
> this is our ENDLESS
> and PROPER WORK.
> **Mary Oliver**

DREAM DIARY

Dream title.

Dream type.

Dream notes.
setting / feelings / objects / people / thoughts / narrative

This dream made me feel...

Question.
What did I do yesterday and how did I feel? Does the dream correlate to my day?

Question.
Does the dream relate to any current themes in my life?

Week 1 Dream Awareness

Day 6 First impressions

Did you remember your dreams last night? Sometimes, upon awakening, dreams begin to fade away quickly. Often, we emerge from the dream world with tantalizing fragments lingering on the edge of consciousness, yet the details remain elusive. It's like our dreams become a mist that is difficult to grasp or capture.

Harnessing first impressions upon awakening is the key to keeping hold of our dreams and subsequently unlocking their deeper meanings. One helpful way to capture those first impressions is to begin to notice and observe your Hypnopompic State, which is the threshold zone you are in right before you wake up.

Hypnopompic: from the Greek words *'hypno-'* meaning *'sleep'* and *'pompic'* derived from *'pompe'*, which means *'sending away'*.

This liminal transition between sleep and wakefulness offers a brief window where dream memories may still be accessible. Upon awakening, remain in a state of relaxed awareness, gently holding onto the remnants of the dream experience before they fade away.

Here's how to do it:

Take a moment of stillness upon waking to allow the dream impressions to settle into your awareness. Close your eyes and gently recollect any images, emotions or sensations that linger from the dream. Avoid rushing into wakeful activities, as this can disrupt the delicate thread connecting you to the dream world.

Keep your dream journal by your bedside and reach for it as soon as you wake up. Write down any fragments, impressions or emotions from the dream, even if they seem vague or disjointed.

Engage your senses to anchor the dream memories in your consciousness. Visualize the dream scenery, recall any sounds or voices heard and evoke the sensations experienced during the dream.

Allow your mind to wander freely and make associations with the dream fragments that arise. Write down any thoughts, memories or associations that come to mind, even if they seem unrelated at first. Trust in the creative flow of your unconscious mind to unveil hidden connections and insights.

DREAM DIARY

Dream title.

Dream type.

Dream notes.
setting / feelings / objects / people / thoughts / narrative

This dream made me feel...

Question.
What did I do yesterday and how did I feel? Does the dream correlate to my day?

Question.
Does the dream relate to any current themes in my life?

Week 1 Dream Awareness

Day 7 Hypnagogic meditation

Yesterday we learned about the hypnopompic state, just before you wake up. Hopefully you were able to try it out this morning. We are now going to explore your threshold state before you fall asleep at night: the hypnagogic.

Hypnopompic: from the Greek words *'hypno-'* meaning 'sleep' and *'-agogic'* derived from *'agōgos'*, which means 'leading'.

The hypnagogic state is the transitional phase between wakefulness and sleep. It occurs as your mind begins to disengage from external stimuli and drifts into the realms of your unconscious.

The hypnagogic state is characterized by a unique blend of sensory experiences, including vivid imagery, fleeting thoughts and auditory hallucinations, often accompanied by a sense of weightlessness or floating. You're going to love it – it's wild!

Let's go for a ride and get you acquainted with your hypnagogic state through a meditation. You can also notice this hypnagogic state just before you go to sleep, which will help you to cultivate your dream awareness.

Hypnagogic meditation:
Sit or lie down in a comfortable position, allowing your body to relax fully. Close your eyes and take a few deep breaths to centre yourself and quiet the mind.

Shift your attention to the sensation of your breath as it flows in and out of your body. Notice the rhythm and depth of each breath, allowing yourself to become fully present in the moment.

As you continue to breathe deeply, consciously release any tension or stress held in the body. Let go of any thoughts or worries, allowing them to drift away like clouds in the sky.

As you relax into the meditation, you may start to notice subtle shifts in consciousness. Embrace the sensations of drifting and floating with gentle curiosity and openness.

As dreamlike images and sensations arise behind your closed eyelids, observe them with detached awareness. Allow the imagery to unfold naturally, without grasping or trying to control the experience. Trust in the wisdom of your unconscious mind to guide you deeper into the realms of dream consciousness.

DREAM DIARY

Dream title.

Dream type.

Dream notes.
setting / feelings / objects / people / thoughts / narrative

This dream made me feel...

Question.
What did I do yesterday and how did I feel? Does the dream correlate to my day?

Question.
Does the dream relate to any current themes in my life?

Week 2

all
in
the

details

Week 2 All in the details

Day 8 Narrative

You are now well on your way with your dream journaling. Congratulations! Dream journaling is an art form that invites you to explore the depths of your unconscious mind and unravel the mysteries of your dream landscape.

At its core, dream journaling is about capturing the essence of your dreams and distilling them into a narrative that reflects the intricate machinations of your inner world.

Dream journaling will become a sacred practice for you. It is a portal through which you can access the wisdom of the unconscious and unleash the poetry of your soul. Your dream journal will become the trusty map of your unconscious worlds. After four weeks of dream journaling, you will be able to read back and get an overview of this fascinating blueprint.

You possess a unique 'dream language', a symbolic lexicon through which your unconscious communicates its messages. Dream journaling allows you to decode this language and uncover the hidden meanings behind your dream imagery, symbols and themes.

One of the keys lies in the narrative of your dream content. Rather than focusing on every minute detail or fragment, strive to identify the overarching storyline or plot that unfolds within your dreams. This narrative serves as a guiding thread, which can lead you deeper into the labyrinth of your unconscious mind.

The narrative of your dreams can provide profound clues into the underlying themes, emotions and patterns that shape your waking reality.

Read through your dream journal so far and:

* Identify key elements.
* Look for patterns.
* Seek out the emotions of your dreams.
* Connect the dots. Is there an overall story?
* Reflect on personal associations.
* Write a summary of the narrative of your dreams.

DREAM DIARY

Dream notes.

Week 2 All in the details

Day 9 Objects

Dream objects are the enigmatic artefacts that populate the landscape of your dreams, imbued with symbolic significance and meaning. These objects can take myriad forms, ranging from everyday items to fantastical creations, and they serve as potent symbols that offer clues into the depths of your unconscious mind.

In the realm of dreamwork, understanding the role of dream objects is crucial for deciphering your personal dream language. Each dream object carries its own unique symbolism and associations, reflecting unconscious wounds, fears, conflicts, trauma, inspiration, creativity, strengths or ambitions that shape your waking reality.

By exploring the meaning of dream objects within the context of your dreams, you can gain valuable insights into your personal mythology – the recurring themes, patterns and narratives that define your individual psyche. Dream objects can also act as signposts along the journey of self-discovery, guiding you towards a deeper understanding of yourself and your place in the world. They are helpers.

Dream objects also provide access to the insightful reservoir of archetypal imagery and symbolism that underpins your dreams.

As you develop your dreamwork practice, you might wish to explore different ways of interpreting symbols. For now, be curious about what they mean for you.

In addition, dream objects can be powerful prompts for lucid dreaming techniques. By recognizing dream objects as symbols of the dream state, you can use them as triggers to become lucid and actively engage with the dream content.

This heightened awareness opens a world of possibilities for exploration and transformation within your dream realm.

Let's find your dream objects. Consider the following questions:

* What objects are appearing in your dreams?
* How do these objects make you feel?
* What do these objects symbolize for you?

DREAM DIARY

Dream title.

Dream type.

Dream notes.
setting / feelings / objects / people / thoughts / narrative

This dream made me feel...

Question.
What did I do yesterday and how did I feel? Does the dream correlate to my day?

Question.
Does the dream relate to any current themes in my life?

Week 2 All in the details

Day 10 Settings

Dream settings, also known as dream architecture, dreamscapes or the dream-a-verse, are the immersive environments in which your dreams unfold. These settings play a crucial role in shaping the narrative and atmosphere of your dreams, providing valuable clues and insights into the workings of your unconscious.

By paying attention to the details of these environments – such as landscapes, buildings or geographical features – you can discover helpful prompts around underlying themes and messages.

Your dream settings may also reflect actual places from your waking life, serving as metaphorical representations of your lived experiences, past memories and inner landscapes. By recognizing familiar settings in your dreams, you can uncover hidden connections between your waking and dreaming realities, shedding light on unresolved issues or unexplored aspects of yourself.

Some dream settings are imbued with a sense of mystery and enchantment and can transport you to otherworldly zones and realms beyond the constraints of time and space. These mystical settings couldn't be more challenging to unpack! Regardless, perhaps these mystical environments are a chance to explore and expand your consciousness in the dream-a-verse and inspire you to return to learn.

Understanding and familiarizing yourself with your dream architecture or dream-scape is also invaluable for cultivating a lucid dreaming practice. In becoming attuned to the unique characteristics and patterns of your dream settings, you can learn to recognize when you are dreaming and become conscious and aware within the dream itself. This heightened awareness opens up a world of possibilities for exploration, transformation, creativity, problem solving and learning, which can encourage you to navigate your dream realm with clarity and intention. Let's explore your dream terrain tonight!

* What settings appear in your dreams?
* How do these various settings make you feel?
* What do these settings symbolize for you?

DREAM DIARY

Dream title.

Dream type.

Dream notes.
setting / feelings / objects / people / thoughts / narrative

This dream made me feel...

Question.
What did I do yesterday and how did I feel? Does the dream correlate to my day?

Question.
Does the dream relate to any current themes in my life?

Week 2 All in the details

Day 11 Emotions

We all get emotional – it's a natural state of being human. For the most part, many of us are taught to curb our emotions or to not burden others with them. However, honouring and processing emotions is key to a healthy and well-balanced happy life.

Your emotions play a crucial role in your overall well-being and regulation. When you suppress or ignore your feelings, they can manifest in various ways, impacting your mental, emotional and physical health. Dreamwork provides a safe and supportive space for exploring and processing emotions, allowing you to release pent-up feelings and achieve greater emotional balance and resilience.

Various emotions popping up in your dreams also serve as a gateway to understanding yourself better and cultivating greater self-awareness. By exploring the emotional landscape of your dreams, you can uncover deep-seated fears, unresolved conflicts and unmet needs that may be influencing your waking life.

When unpacking the emotional content of your dreams, they can also help you navigate life's challenges with greater ease and grace. Leaning into the practice of recognizing and honouring your emotions, you will be able to cultivate healthier coping strategies and develop greater resilience in the face of adversity.

So, have no fear of the depths of the emotional realms within you. Your emotions are powerful allies in an immersive journey of self-discovery, healing, transformation and self-realization. Let's dive in!

* Consider a recurring dream that you have experienced.
* Feel into the dream and sense what emotions are at the core of this dream.
* What do these emotions symbolize for you?
* How do these emotions relate to your waking life?

DREAM DIARY

Dream title.

Dream type.

Dream notes.
setting / feelings / objects / people / thoughts / narrative

This dream made me feel...

Question.
What did I do yesterday and how did I feel? Does the dream correlate to my day?

Question.
Does the dream relate to any current themes in my life?

Dreamwork

Week 2 **All in the details**

Day 12 **People**

Who are you dreaming about? At times, dreams can feel busy and sociable and particular people can emerge or a diverse cast of characters might feature, representing common and significant themes. Being mindful of the people who appear in your dreams can direct you towards hidden messages, symbols and archetypes.

When reflecting on a dream about a specific person, it's important to consider the role they play and the emotions they evoke. Each person in your dreams may represent different aspects of yourself or reflect significant relationships, dynamics or experiences from your waking life.

People in dreams may also represent archetypes – universal symbols and patterns of behaviour that are deeply ingrained in the collective unconscious. Archetypes, as defined by Swiss psychiatrist Carl Jung, are primordial images and themes that recur across cultures and time periods, representing fundamental aspects of the human experience. By recognizing the archetypal qualities embodied by dream characters, you can discover the broader themes and narratives at play within your dreams.

❝❞
In JUNGIAN theory, an archetype is a primitive mental image inherited from the EARLIEST HUMAN ANCESTORS, and supposed to be present in the COLLECTIVE UNCONSCIOUS.
Oxford Dictionary

In some cases, the appearance of a specific person in a dream may be literal, reflecting our thoughts, feelings or interactions with that person in waking life. I see these dream appearances as a nudge to perhaps get in touch with the person. Many times, I have listened to my dream prompts about people and have found them to be synchronous, helpful and healing both to myself and the person involved. Who are you connecting to in your dreams?

DREAM DIARY

Dream title.

Dream type.

Dream notes.
setting / feelings / objects / people / thoughts / narrative

This dream made me feel...

Question.
What did I do yesterday and how did I feel? Does the dream correlate to my day?

Question.
Does the dream relate to any current themes in my life?

Week 2 All in the details

Day 13 Recurring patterns

Recurring patterns in dreams serve as potent messages from our unconscious realms, asking us to pay attention to specific themes, issues or experiences that require our conscious awareness.

I like to see these repetitive patterns as prompts: something in the unconscious that is giving us consistent nudges to do the inner work around a particular theme.

By identifying and reflecting on recurring patterns in dreams, you can begin to unravel the underlying messages and meanings they contain. These patterns often point to specific areas of our waking life where we may be stuck, stagnant or resistant to change. They serve as invitations to explore and confront the shadow aspects of ourselves – the parts of our psyche that we may deny, suppress or disown.

Recurring patterns in dreams want to set us free from the grip of unconscious patterns and conditioning that hold us back from realizing our full potential. They offer opportunities for growth, healing and transformation by shining a light on the areas of our lives where we may be out of alignment with our true selves.

By paying attention to recurring patterns in dreams and engaging in introspection and reflection, we can begin to break free from the limitations of the past and embrace the fullness of our being. These patterns serve as catalysts for personal growth and evolution, guiding us towards greater self-awareness, authenticity and fulfilment. Recurring dreams are our teachers, healers and guides!

Consider the following questions:

* What are your recurring dreams or themes?
* How do these dreams make you feel?
* What are your recurring dreams telling you?

Pause for reflection:
Make a note of it.

DREAM DIARY

Dream title.

Dream type.

Dream notes.
setting / feelings / objects / people / thoughts / narrative

This dream made me feel...

Question.
What did I do yesterday and how did I feel? Does the dream correlate to my day?

Question.
Does the dream relate to any current themes in my life?

Week 2 All in the details

Day 14 Seeing from different angles: a meditation

When engaging in dreamwork, it's crucial to approach dreams from multiple angles and perspectives. Each vantage point offers unique insights and clues that contribute to a deeper understanding of the dream's meaning and significance. By exploring different perspectives, you can begin to unravel the layers of symbolism, emotion and narrative woven into the fabric of your dreams.

A helpful approach to exploring different vantage points in dreamwork is through the Gestalt dream work method. In the 1940s, Fritz Perls, Laura Perls, and Paul Goodman created Gestalt therapy, emphasizing personal responsibility, present-moment awareness and integrating conflicting aspects of the self. This approach highlights the importance of engaging with different aspects of the dream as if they are parts of yourself or representatives of your psyche.

In Gestalt dream work, you can interact with different elements of the dream through role-playing, dialogue or visualization techniques. By embodying different perspectives within the dream, you can gain greater clarity and insight into the underlying dynamics at play and uncover hidden aspects of yourself that seek integration and wholeness.

One method for accessing different vantage points with the Gestalt method is through meditation. Let's try it out.

Find a quiet and comfortable space where you can relax and focus your attention inwards. Close your eyes and take several deep breaths, allowing your body and mind to settle into a state of calm and receptivity. As you continue to breathe deeply, visualize yourself stepping back from the dream scene and observing it from a distance. Notice any details or patterns that emerge from this new vantage point, allowing yourself to gain a broader perspective on the dream's content and symbolism.

Imagine yourself stepping into the dream and experiencing it from the perspective of each character or element within the dream. Notice how each perspective offers unique insights and emotions, allowing you to deepen your understanding of the dream's themes and messages.

DREAM DIARY

Dream title.

Dream type.

Dream notes.
setting / feelings / objects / people / thoughts / narrative

This dream made me feel...

Question.
What did I do yesterday and how did I feel? Does the dream correlate to my day?

Question.
Does the dream relate to any current themes in my life?

Dreamwork

Week 3

dream

Week 3 Dream Guides

Day 15 Integrating dreams into daily life

You've entered week three of your journey and you have a record of many of your dreams to work with now! Moving forward, it is time to start integrating these dreams into your daily life. This is a transformative practice that can allow you to harness the wisdom of your dreams and apply this wisdom in your waking reality. Through integration, you bridge the gap between your dream world and your waking world: unlocking profound insights, cultivating self-awareness and navigating life's challenges with greater clarity and purpose.

A central theme in Carl Jung's psychology is that dreamwork is deeply intertwined with the concept of individuation. Individuation refers to the process of becoming whole and realizing one's true self. Dreams, according to Jung, play a crucial role in this journey.

The more you engage in integrating your dreams, the more you become attuned to the messages of your dreams and the patterns within them. This process of dream exploration, reflection and integration will gradually lead you towards greater self-awareness of the different aspects of the psyche. You then move closer to realizing your unique potential and begin to achieve a sense of wholeness – the ultimate goal of individuation.

One helpful tip for integrating dreams into your daily life is to stay rooted in your dream journaling practice (which you've been doing, so keep it up!). Reading back and reflecting on your dreams and their relevance to your waking life is an important foundation that provides valuable guidance and inspiration for your personal growth and transformation.

Another technique for integrating dreams with daily life is to engage in active imagination or visualization exercises. Set aside time each day to revisit significant dream imagery or symbols, allowing yourself to immerse fully in the dream experience. Explore the meaning and significance of these symbols and consider how they might apply to your current life circumstances or challenges. Read back through your dream journal and choose a dream:

* Make a drawing of the dream opposite.
* What is the dream telling you?
* How can you apply this in your waking life?

DREAM DIARY

Drawing space.

Week 3 Dream Guides

Day 16 Dream bridging

How were your dreams last night? Hopefully you have been making the connections between your dreams and your waking life and now you can move forwards applying the lessons from your dreams to your daily life. A great way to help you continue to connect-the-dots and integrate is through the wonderful occurrence of synchronicity.

Synchronicity, a term coined by Jung, refers to meaningful coincidences that occur in your life, seemingly unrelated events or occurrences that are connected by their significance and timing. We all remember a synchronicity that has occurred in our life. Those uncanny coincidences that often surprise us, bring wonderment and can feel like a mystical experience. In the context of dreamwork, synchronicity suggests that the symbols, themes and events that appear in our dreams can also appear as synchronistic patterns unfolding in our waking lives.

By paying attention to synchronistic connections between your dreams and waking experiences, you can experience eureka moments concerning the underlying dynamics at play in your life. Through embracing synchronicities, you can also uncover hidden patterns and meanings that may be influencing your thoughts, feelings, behaviours or personal journey towards individuation.

One technique for finding connections between dreams and waking life is dream-bridging, a process that involves exploring the parallels and resonances between dream imagery and experiences in your daily life. Let's create the bridge!

Read back in your dream journal and reflect:

* Can you identify any themes, symbols or emotions?
* Have these themes, symbols or emotions. appeared in waking reality?
* What synchronicities have you experienced?

DREAM DIARY

Dream title.

Dream type.

Dream notes.
setting / feelings / objects / people / thoughts / narrative

This dream made me feel...

Question.
What did I do yesterday and how did I feel? Does the dream correlate to my day?

Question.
Does the dream relate to any current themes in my life?

Week 3 Dream Guides

Day 17 Intuition & premonition

Intuition and premonition are powerful phenomena that often intersect with dreams and dreamwork, offering glimpses into the deeper mysteries of the realms of the unconscious, the collective unconscious and the interconnectedness of the universe.

Intuition, often described as a gut feeling or inner knowing, is the ability to understand or perceive something instinctively, without the need for conscious reasoning. Premonition, on the other hand, involves foreknowledge or forewarning of future events, often experienced as a vivid dream or sudden insight.

In the realm of dreams and dreamwork, intuition and premonition play a significant role in guiding and informing your understanding of your dream experience. Dreams are a fertile ground for intuition to flourish, as they provide a direct line of communication between the conscious and unconscious aspects of your psyche. Through dreams, you may receive intuitive insights, guidance or warnings that illuminate your path and offer valuable wisdom for navigating life's challenges and opportunities.

Similarly, premonitions can manifest in dreams as vivid and prophetic visions of future events or outcomes. While the nature of premonitions remains mysterious and often elusive, many people report experiencing premonitory dreams that foreshadow significant events or circumstances in their lives. These dreams may serve as wake-up calls or opportunities for preparation, allowing you to anticipate and respond to future developments with greater awareness and foresight. Simply put, these types of dreams are here to help us and others!

Here is how you can deepen your intuition and activate premonition dreams: listen to your inner voice, practice mindfulness, reflect on past hunches, tune into your body, spend time in nature, stay open-minded and set an evening intention to activate intuition and premonition.

Read back through your dream journal and reflect:

* Can you identify any intuitive or premonitory dreams?
* How did it apply to your waking reality?
* What is your dream mantra tonight?

DREAM DIARY

Dream title.

Dream type.

Dream notes.
setting / feelings / objects / people / thoughts / narrative

This dream made me feel...

Question.
What did I do yesterday and how did I feel? Does the dream correlate to my day?

Question.
Does the dream relate to any current themes in my life?

Week 3 Dream Guides

Day 18 Symbolism

How was your intuitive dreaming last night? Hopefully it was full of rich symbolism to unpack! Dream symbolism operates on multiple levels, ranging from personal and cultural associations to archetypal patterns and universal themes. Personal symbols in dreams often reflect those experiences, memories and associations that are unique to your life. These symbols may hold deeply personal meanings that are specific to you.

Cultural symbols, on the other hand, are influenced by the collective beliefs, values and myths of our society or community. These symbols may vary across different cultures and contexts, reflecting shared experiences, traditions and beliefs that shape the collective psyche. By noticing cultural symbols in dreams, you can gain a deeper understanding of the broader social and cultural influences that shape your perceptions and experiences.

There are also archetypal symbols that pop up in your dreams too. Archetypes, as defined by Jung, are universal patterns and themes that recur across cultures and time periods. These archetypal symbols, such as the heroine, the shadow or the wise old woman, represent fundamental aspects of your human experience and also serve as reflections of the collective unconscious. By exploring archetypal symbols in your dreams, you can tap into the deeper layers of the psyche and uncover universal truths and insights that transcend individual differences. It can be boundary dissolving!

Here is how you can begin to identify your dream symbols: pay attention to symbols or themes that appear frequently in your dreams, reflect on your personal associations with each dream symbol, research the cultural or archetypal meanings of your dream symbols and take note of how the symbol makes you feel.

> **❝❞**
> MYTHS AND DREAMS come from the SAME PLACE.
> **Joseph Campbell**

DREAM DIARY

Dream title.

Dream type.

Dream notes.
setting / feelings / objects / people / thoughts / narrative

This dream made me feel...

Question.
What did I do yesterday and how did I feel? Does the dream correlate to my day?

Question.
Does the dream relate to any current themes in my life?

Dreamwork

Week 3 Dream Guides

Day 19 Guides in your dreams: how they often show up

When guides appear in dreams, they serve as valuable companions and mentors on your journey through your unconscious realms, offering guidance, wisdom and support as you navigate the landscape of your psyche.

One common form of guides in dreams is animals – they are often associated with instinct, intuition and primal wisdom. Animals may appear in dreams as spirit guides or power animals, offering guidance and protection, or as symbols of specific qualities or attributes that they are encouraging you to embody or cultivate.

Ancestors are another powerful form of guides in dreams, representing the wisdom and legacy of those who have come before us. Ancestral guides may appear in dreams to offer guidance, healing or support or to convey important messages or lessons from the past.

Dream characters, such as friends, family members or strangers can also serve as guides in dreams, appearing to offer insight, guidance or assistance in navigating the challenges or opportunities presented within the dream narrative.

Dream guides can also get a bit mystical too! Elementals, angels, deities, mythical creatures or spiritual beings could pop up in dreams to teach or offer divine guidance, protection, healing, enlightenment or to convey messages of hope, inspiration or transformation.

When guides appear frequently in your dreams, it is important to pay attention, as they may be trying to convey important messages or teach valuable lessons.

You can set your intention to connect with your guides before you go to sleep and visualize them as you are drifting off. And you can foster these relationships by expressing gratitude for their presence and guidance.

Read back through your dream journal and reflect:

* Can you identify any dream guides?
* How does the dream guide make you feel?
* What is their message to you?
* How can you apply this to your waking life?
* What is your dream mantra tonight?

DREAM DIARY

Dream title.

Dream type.

Dream notes.
setting / feelings / objects / people / thoughts / narrative

This dream made me feel…

Question.
What did I do yesterday and how did I feel? Does the dream correlate to my day?

Question.
Does the dream relate to any current themes in my life?

Week 3 Dream Guides

Day 20 **Problem-solving**

When you are dreaming, your unconscious mind is free to explore unconventional ideas, associations and possibilities that may not be readily apparent in waking consciousness.

You can gain fresh perspectives, innovative approaches and novel solutions to complex problems, tapping into the limitless potential of your creative imagination.

Your dreams can also facilitate problem-solving by providing a safe space for experimentation and exploration, allowing you to test out different scenarios, strategies and solutions in a dream environment before implementing them in your waking life.

By engaging with dreams in this way, you can gain valuable feedback, clarity and confidence in their decision-making process, leading to more effective outcomes.

The phrase 'Let me sleep on it' is often used when faced with an important decision and it holds some truth! It's a known process called 'dream incubation'. This technique is thousands of years old and found its origins in Ancient Greece where the practice of focusing intention on a specific question, issue or problem before going to sleep was part of everyday life. It was taken so seriously by the Greeks that they built 'sleep temples' called Asclepions, devoted to the practice of dream incubation.

By setting an intention to receive guidance or insight in your dreams before you fall asleep, you can not only tap into your unconscious zones but also tap into the collective unconscious which holds a vast reservoir of knowledge and creativity, allowing solutions to emerge organically during your dream states.

How to practice dream incubation:
Set an intention, implement it into your nightly ritual, draw and read about your intention before sleep, visualize your intention on the threshold of sleep and repeat your dream mantra.

Dream incubation may not yield immediate results, so be patient and persistent in your practice. It may take several nights or weeks of consistent effort before you begin to experience dreams related to your intention.

DREAM DIARY

Dream title.

Dream type.

Dream notes.
setting / feelings / objects / people / thoughts / narrative

This dream made me feel...

Question.
What did I do yesterday and how did I feel? Does the dream correlate to my day?

Question.
Does the dream relate to any current themes in my life?

Dreamwork

Week 3 Dream Guides

Day 21 A meditation for asking your dreams to channel your higher self

You are an amazing being! There is an aspect of you called the 'higher self' which is part of your consciousness that is in tune with universal truths, divine wisdom and the interconnectedness of all beings. It is the source of your inner guidance, inspiration and intuition, offering insights and perspectives that transcend the limitations of your ego and rational mind.

Your higher self resides at a higher level of consciousness, beyond the realm of your everyday thoughts, emotions and perceptions. It is considered to be the true essence of your being, representing the soul or spirit that exists beyond the physical body and the material world.

Here is a nightly meditation to help you effectively communicate with your higher self through your dreams:

Create a peaceful and relaxed atmosphere before bedtime by engaging in calming activities such as meditation, deep breathing, or gentle stretching. Clear your mind of any distractions or worries and open yourself to receiving guidance from your higher self.

Bedtime calming ritual:

Before going to sleep, take a few moments to set a clear intention to connect with your higher self in your dreams. State your intention aloud or write it down to reinforce your commitment.

On the threshold of sleep, visualize your higher self in your mind's eye. Imagine yourself surrounded by light and love, embodying your highest potential and wisdom.

Directly address your higher self in your mind. Ask for guidance, clarity and insight in your dreams. Be specific about the areas of your life or questions you seek guidance on.

Tomorrow, reflect on your dreams and any messages or symbols that may have been communicated by your higher self. Consider how they relate to your waking life and what guidance they may offer. Write down your findings.

Connecting with your higher self through your dreams may not happen overnight, so be patient and persistent in your practice. Trust that your higher self is always available to guide and support you, even if it takes time to receive clear messages.

DREAM DIARY

Dream title.

Dream type.

Dream notes.
setting / feelings / objects / people / thoughts / narrative

This dream made me feel...

Question.
What did I do yesterday and how did I feel? Does the dream correlate to my day?

Question.
Does the dream relate to any current themes in my life?

Week 4

deeper
conscio

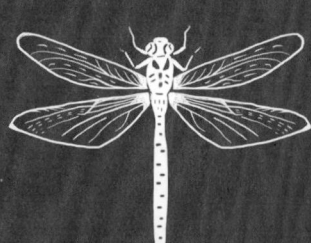

er

usness

Week 4 Deeper consciousness

Day 22 Self-reflection: a window into the soul

You've been on quite a journey these past three weeks! It's time for a bit of self-reflection. This is a fundamental aspect of dreamwork, offering a pathway to deeper understanding, insight and personal growth through the exploration of your dreams, thoughts and emotions.

By reflecting on your dream journey, you will gain some perspectives and insights about your waking reality. Perhaps you will even uncover connections, parallels and synchronicities that offer guidance, validation and inspiration for your personal growth and transformation.

A great way to engage in self-reflection is through meditation and journaling. Let's give it a try!

Begin by taking a few deep breaths to centre yourself and quiet your mind. As you breathe in, imagine inhaling calm and clarity and as you exhale, imagine releasing tension and stress.

Reflect on your journey into your dreams. What experiences did you have? What emotions did it bring up for you? How did you evolve, heal or grow?

Consider the lessons you've learned from this experience. What insights have you gained about yourself, your strengths and areas for growth?

Visualize yourself stepping into your power and embracing the lessons learned from your dreams.

Now, shift your focus to your goals and aspirations. What are you working towards in your dreams now? What steps can you take to move closer to achieving them?

Reflect on any limiting beliefs or self-doubt that may be holding you back from reaching your full potential. How can you gently challenge these beliefs and cultivate a mindset of confidence and self-belief?

Take a moment to express gratitude for the progress you've made and the lessons you've learned along the way. What are you grateful for at this moment?

Close your meditation by setting an intention for your dreams tonight.

DREAM DIARY

Dream title.

Dream type.

Dream notes.
setting / feelings / objects / people / thoughts / narrative

This dream made me feel...

Question.
What did I do yesterday and how did I feel? Does the dream correlate to my day?

Question.
Does the dream relate to any current themes in my life?

Week 4 Deeper consciousness

Day 23 Dreams & creativity

Dreams have long been recognized as a wellspring of creativity, providing fertile ground for inspiration, imagination and innovation. Moreover, dreams can spark the creative process by offering fresh perspectives, alternative realities and novel ideas that challenge conventional thinking and expand the boundaries of imagination.

Over the last three weeks, you've been preparing yourself for a deeper dive into dreams and creativity by setting the foundations of dream journaling, dream integration and dream incubation. You've been doing so well!

Now, in this fourth week, after revisiting your dreams and reflecting on their content, imagery and deeper meanings, we can spark some creativity and ignite your imagination.

> **The POWER of the IMAGINATION makes us INFINITE.**
> John Muir

A creative method I love to guide my students and clients towards is using art and drawing for dream integration. This can be a powerful way to deepen your understanding of your dreams. By visually representing dream imagery, emotions and symbols, you can access aspects of your unconscious realms that may be more challenging to articulate verbally.

Through the creative process, you can explore the nuances of your dreams, uncover hidden meanings, receive revelations and connect the dots. Art offers a non-linear, intuitive approach to dreamwork, allowing for a rich and personal exploration of the dream landscape. Plus, you create an intriguing work of art that can remind you of your integrative journey towards individuation and empowerment.

DREAM DIARY

Dream title.

Dream type.

Dream notes.
setting / feelings / objects / people / thoughts / narrative

This dream made me feel...

Question.
What did I do yesterday and how did I feel? Does the dream correlate to my day?

Question.
Does the dream relate to any current themes in my life?

Dreamwork

Week 4 Deeper consciousness

Day 24 Times of transition

Whether you are experiencing affirming or challenging transitions in your life, dreams can serve as a source of wisdom, clarity and resilience, helping you to steer through the waters of uncertainty, cope with change and find meaning and direction on your journey.

Affirming life transitions may include rites of passage such as marriage, parenthood, career advancement or personal growth and self-discovery. During these times, dreams can offer encouragement, validation and inspiration, providing insights and guidance for embracing new opportunities, nurturing relationships and pursuing goals and aspirations. Take note of the symbolism, imagery and emotions present in your dreams even during positive landmarks in your life. They can help you gain clarity and confidence as you journey through these transformative periods.

And of course, life has its challenging chapters too: loss, death, illness, divorce or career setbacks can be particularly challenging to navigate. However, dreams can offer solace, comfort and healing during these difficult times, providing opportunities for processing grief, exploring emotions and finding resilience and strength.

If you are currently going through a transition, take a little time to reflect on it and how it makes you feel. How might the transition currently be showing up in your dreams in symbols, settings or the types of dreams you are having?

Set an intention to receive guidance in your dreams, and on the threshold of sleep visualize yourself successfully navigating the transition and repeat your dream mantra.

> **❝❞**
> Until you make the
> UNCONSCIOUS CONSCIOUS,
> it will direct your life
> and you WILL CALL IT FATE.
> **Carl Jung**

DREAM DIARY

Dream title.

Dream type.

Dream notes.
setting / feelings / objects / people / thoughts / narrative

This dream made me feel...

Question.
What did I do yesterday and how did I feel? Does the dream correlate to my day?

Question.
Does the dream relate to any current themes in my life?

Week 4 Deeper consciousness

Day 25 Wisdom of the shadow

Just as your dreams will reflect times of change, growth and healing, they also shine a light into the parts of you that are hidden in your waking life. The term 'shadow', popularized by Jung, is the wounded aspect of yourself: the aspect of yourself that you repress, deny or reject. The shadow also represents the unconscious aspects of your personality, including your fears, insecurities, suppressed desires and unresolved emotions.

Dreams offer a unique opportunity to work with the shadow, as by paying attention to the more uncomfortable elements of your dreams you can begin to identify your shadow and therefore initiate the process of integrating it into your conscious awareness. By exploring the shadow aspects of your dreams, you can uncover hidden patterns, beliefs and emotions that may be influencing

> ❝❞
> You MUST GO into the DARK in order to bring forth YOUR LIGHT.
> Debbie Ford

your thoughts, behaviours and relationships in waking life. This self-awareness can then allow you to take responsibility for your shadow and work towards healing and integration.

This process of emotional healing can allow you to move towards wholeness and authenticity, aligning with your true self and living a more fulfilling and meaningful life. It is on-going work, so take this journey at your own pace. When you are ready to explore the darker aspects of your dreams, that's when you are really allowing your dreams to help you heal and grow.

Read through your dream journal and identify a dream that was uncomfortable for you. Or perhaps you have a recurring dream that you can now explore. If you can identify it, what is your shadow telling you through the dream?

DREAM DIARY

Dream title.

Dream type.

Dream notes.
setting / feelings / objects / people / thoughts / narrative

This dream made me feel...

Question.
What did I do yesterday and how did I feel? Does the dream correlate to my day?

Question.
Does the dream relate to any current themes in my life?

Week 4 Deeper consciousness

Day 26 Manifesting

Manifestation is a bit of a buzzword these days but there is some deep truth to it. The power of dreams to manifest your reality, shaping and influencing the world around you through the creative power of your unconscious mind is an exciting potential.

Drawing upon ancient wisdom and modern teachings, you can harness the transformative prospect of your dreams to manifest your desires, goals and aspirations in your waking life. And guess what? You have already been paving the way for manifestation through your consistent evening intentions!

By setting evening intentions, visualizing outcomes, and engaging in dreamwork practices, you can eventually manifest your goals within the dream which, in turn, plants the seeds of intention that can manifest in your waking life. Let's start manifesting!

Here is how you can begin manifesting through your dreams:

* Find your goal.
* Feel the excitement.
* Visualize or draw your goal as a symbol.
* Focus on your symbol and all the positive feelings connected to it.
* On the threshold of sleep conjure your symbol and excitement and repeat your dream mantra.

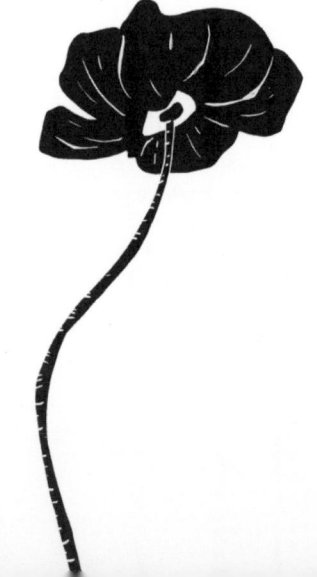

DREAM DIARY

Dream title.

Dream type.

Dream notes.
setting / feelings / objects / people / thoughts / narrative

This dream made me feel...

Question.
What did I do yesterday and how did I feel? Does the dream correlate to my day?

Question.
Does the dream relate to any current themes in my life?

Dreamwork

Week 4 Deeper consciousness

Day 27 First steps to lucid dreaming

Well, my friend, it's almost time for the big send off and I want to introduce you to the concept of lucid dreaming. This fascinating dream phenomenon is when you become aware that you are dreaming while still in the middle of a dream.

In lucid dreams, the dreamer is conscious and can often exert some degree of control over the dream environment, characters and narrative.

This heightened state of awareness offers a unique opportunity for exploration, creativity and personal growth within the realm of dreams.

The first stepi s to cultivate a greater awareness of your dreams. You've been doing this over the last four weeks by recording your dreams in your journal, identifying your dream symbols, setting intentions, repeating dream mantras, engaging in dream incubation and more.

Additionally, practising reality checks throughout the day – such as looking at your hands, questioning your surroundings or trying to remember how you got where you are – can help you establish the habit of questioning your waking reality, which can carry over into your dreams.

It's important to approach lucid dreaming with patience, persistence and an open mind. While some dreamers may experience lucid dreams spontaneously, for others, it may take time and practise to develop the skills and awareness necessary to induce lucidity.

Make yourself a cup of dream tea, such as Mugwort. Engage in dream incubation activities like reading a book on lucid dreaming, drawing, journaling or meditating.

On the threshold of sleep visualize yourself becoming lucid in your dream tonight. Imagine yourself finding a particular dream symbol such as a crystal or an animal, questioning your reality and gaining awareness within the dream. Visualize yourself exploring the dream world with clarity and control.

Repeat your dream mantra on the threshold of sleep. Observe the hypnagogic state for as long as your consciousness can as your body falls into sleep...

DREAM DIARY

Dream title.

Dream type.

Dream notes.
setting / feelings / objects / people / thoughts / narrative

This dream made me feel...

Question.
What did I do yesterday and how did I feel? Does the dream correlate to my day?

Question.
Does the dream relate to any current themes in my life?

Dreamwork

Week 4 **Deeper consciousness**

Day 28 **Integration**

First, let me congratulate you on reaching the end of your four-week dreamwork journey. On this final day, we're going to focus on integration, a crucial step in making sense of all the insights and wisdom you've gathered. It's about processing and applying these dream messages to initiate positive change in your life.

Integration is like weaving a tapestry; it's where you collect all the colourful threads of your nightly visions and create a coherent picture. It's essential because it allows you to transform the raw material of your dreams into actionable insights. Without it, dreams remain just interesting stories or abstract symbols. The true power of dreamwork lies in how you apply these messages to your waking life, guiding you towards growth, healing and self-discovery.

Reflective Exercise for Dream Integration

Find a peaceful spot where you feel at ease. Light a candle or play some soft, calming music if that helps you relax. Take a few deep breaths to centre yourself.

Take your dream journal and spend some time flipping through the entries from the past four weeks. As you read, highlight or note any recurring themes, symbols or messages that stand out to you.

Now, think about how you can apply the insights from your dreams to your daily life. Write down practical steps you can take. This could be changing a habit, addressing a fear, pursuing a passion, or simply being more mindful of certain aspects of your life.

Summarise your insights and intentions opposite in a few sentences. For example: 'Over the past four weeks, my dreams have shown me the importance of self-care and setting boundaries. Moving forward, I will make time for myself daily and assert my needs with kindness and confidence.'

Close your eyes and take a few moments to visualize yourself integrating these insights into your life. See yourself living out the changes and embracing the wisdom your dreams have provided.

Finally, express gratitude for the journey you've been on and for the messages your dreams have given you. Thank your unconscious mind for its guidance and support. **Trust in the journey and I'll see you in your dreams!**

DREAM DIARY

Information

About Tree

Tree is a published author and TEDx speaker who works in the field of Transpersonal Psychology with a focus on dreams and death. She is a graduate of the Alef Trust in their programme for Transpersonal Psychology and is a CPD Crossfields Institute Certified Death Doula.

Tree is active in creating a community around dream exploration, offering online courses, retreats, speaking events, 1:1 sessions and maintaining a presence on social media where she shares tips, and experiences, and engages with a broader audience interested in dreams and consciousness exploration.

Instagram @tree_carr
www.luciddreamtree.com

Information:
First published:
Inner Work Project, 2024
Text copyright ©
Tree Carr 2024

All rights reserved.
ISBN 978-1-916563-03-2
Graphic Design:
Supafrank

Printed in the UK by Pureprint.

Discover more workbooks to put your good intentions into daily practice.

www.innerworkproject.com